Permeate & PENETRATE

Permeate & PENETRATE

Trauma and Reformulation Poetry

TERRIANN WALLING

and

GEORGE GERARD

Copyright © 2016 by Terriann Walling and George Gerard

All rights reserved. This book or any portion thereof may not be reproduced or used in any manner whatsoever without the express written permission of the publisher except for the use of brief quotations in a book review or scholarly journal.

First Printing: 2017

ISBN: 978-0-9959845-0-9

Purple Fire Publications
343 Bentham Crescent
Saskatoon, Saskatchewan, S7N3V2
Canada

to the whimsical, wondrous, and those that whisper

era uoy ohw wonk uoy

CONTENTS

Trauma & Reformulation Poetry

1. TRAUMA IN OUR CONTEMPORARY TIME	3
2. A TORRENT OF BROKEN IMAGES: CONSTANT PENETRATION OF COLLECTIVE TRAUMAS	7
3. A MOSAIC RESPONSE	11
4. THE FOUNDATIONS OF REFORMULATION POETRY	15
Literary Trauma Theory	16
The Crying Wound	20
Testimonial Poetry	25
Witnessing & An Address	28
Reformulation	33

The Reformulation Process: *How to Create a Mosaic*

THE PROCESS	39

Testimonies & Reformulated Poems

TESTIMONY - REFORMULATION SET #1	51
TESTIMONY - REFORMULATION SET #2	55
TESTIMONY - REFORMULATION SET #3	61
TESTIMONY - REFORMULATION SET #4	65
TESTIMONY - REFORMULATION SET #5	71
TESTIMONY - REFORMULATION SET #6	77
TESTIMONY - REFORMULATION SET #7	81

Interviews & Concluding Thoughts

1. INTERVIEWS	89
2. CONCLUDING THOUGHTS	99

CONTENTS

Notes   101
Photos   107
Index   109

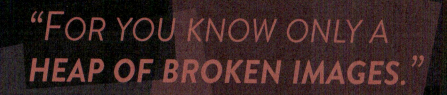

Trauma & Reformulation Poetry

TRAUMA IN OUR CONTEMPORARY TIME

*T*rauma is a fundamental human experience. Damaging events in individual's lives occur at collective and personal levels and produce traumas that are embedded within the psyche. Rooted traumas can be accessed and redefined through the

KEY PIECES

> Layered fragmentation is the compiling of past and present traumas in each person.

> The theory of reformulation poetry is a collaborative process that deconstructs traumatic poetry and reforms responses of meaning in a new poem.

theory of *reformulation poetry*. Literary trauma theory and twentieth century poetry can be adapted to the twenty-first century predicament of layered fragmentation. In the 1922 poem, *The Waste Land*, T.S. Eliot predicted that a future broken society would be resurrected from a "dead land [consisting of individuals] mixing / Memory and desire, stirring / Dull roots with spring rain".[1]

DEAD LAND MIXING
MEMORY AND DESIRE, STIRRING
DULL ROOTS WITH SPRING RAIN

In ways, Eliot's prediction is ominously true; April has bred a wasteland peoples made up of broken images compiled of exposure to collective traumatic events layered upon personal traumas. The digital revolution has increased the penetration of collective traumatic events. Humans are exponentially bombarded with heaps of broken images that are projected faster than can be cognitively addressed. Personal traumas interweave with the collective, making each human a disjointed pile of fragments. The twenty-first century has fostered a pace that has rarely allowed individuals to emerge from underneath the fragmented layers. There is a false sense that compartmentalization is needed to rationalize human existence. Society is shackled by trauma. Helplessness is bred in the confusion of broken images that flash like lights when looking out of a window on a subway train.

*How do we **make a mosaic** from these heaps of broken images rather than letting them build into a wasteland from which we can never escape?*

Reformulation poetry allows individuals to access the wounds of their traumas and amalgamates them through a collaborative process. The process uses the actions of giving testimony, witnessing another's wounds, and responding to the address of the testimony as a method to understand trauma. Reformulation poetry is an addition to these actions. It combines two individual testimonies into a single reformed poem. It is the creation of a mosaic from broken images, and in the act of creation, the voice of a needed response can be heard with a new strength and empowerment that can redefine the future.

A TORRENT OF BROKEN IMAGES

CONSTANT PENETRATION OF COLLECTIVE TRAUMAS

Collective traumas are the foundational fragments of humanity. The broken images of an unaddressed reality must be viewed through the lens of historical recognition and understood relative to the advancements of the current day. Collective traumas, such as

KEY PIECES

> Collective traumas are foundational fragments that have shaped humanity throughout history.

> Technology has provided a common shared experience of collective trauma.

> Personal trauma cannot escape collective trauma.

constant wars, patriarchal dominance, and colonial subjugation have shaped society through the pursuit of power. Fragmented history has compiled exponentially through an increased collective visibility of catastrophic events. The emergence of the moving picture uniquely transformed the experience of connectivity; from the big screen to the small screen, television sets were introduced into the household and became a common shared experience. At times, horrific events and stories were broadcasted into people's homes without understanding the implications of witnessing trauma at a rapidly shared scale.

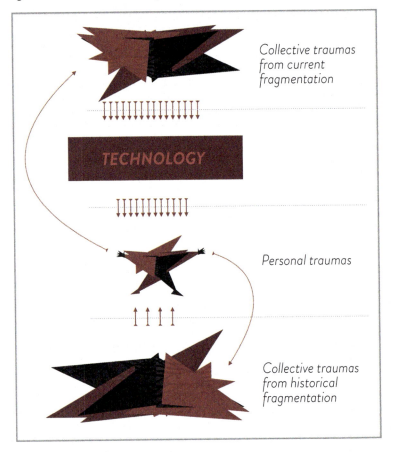

A prime example of this collective penetration, through television, is the event of terror that occurred on September 11, 2001. 9/11 has been well documented, and it was a tragic event that profoundly impacted the world. In 2009, results from a national longitudinal study on the effects of the collective trauma of 9/11, were published in a paper titled *Searching for and Finding Meaning in Collective Trauma: Results From a National Longitudinal Study of the 9/11 Terrorist Attacks* by John A.

Updegraff, Roxane Cohen Silver, and E. Alison Holman. In it they write,

> Tens of thousands of individuals saw firsthand the attacks on the World Trade Center (WTC) and the Pentagon. Even more individuals were shaken by vivid and pervasive television images—either viewed live or within minutes after the attacks. Although the psychological impact was greatest among New York City residents[1], the psychological effects of 9/11 spread far wider than the epicenters. In the days following the attacks, nearly half of Americans reported symptoms of posttraumatic stress[2], and many of these symptoms remained elevated in the following weeks and months[3]. Even more common were fears of additional terrorist attacks, as more than half of Americans had ongoing concerns for the safety of themselves and their families[4],[5]

9/11's events were viewed globally, primarily through televised broadcasts, and they have had a pronounced psychological impact which still permeates today. When a trauma such as 9/11 is left unresolved, the shock of exposure can lead to responsive actions that do not mentally encode in a way that will help an individual find meaning. Horrific events across the world continue to occur and remain unaddressed. New advancements in smart devices and media frameworks provide wide-ranging access to visual and auditory experiences. The piling of fragmented images, within the collective consciousness, has increased through the rapid exposure of catastrophic imagery found in new online platforms that virally socialize events. As an event gains in virality, replication across social sites increases the momentum of exposure. Response to digital takedown requests to hide graphic trauma can be slow, and one is penetrated with unwanted images. This penetration is constant and nearly unstoppable. In the twenty-first century, this has led to shattered individuals that are compiled of ancestral, individual, and collective traumas.

COMPILED FRAGMENTS CAN BE RECOGNIZED AND REFORMED INTO A MOSAIC.

A MOSAIC RESPONSE

𝒜 physical mosaic is a collection of pieces, such as stones or broken fragments that are used to create new patterns or images. A mosaic redefines the purpose of each individual piece by reforming them into an addressed, and actively cognitive, organized image. Fragments of trauma are direct reflections of the first ununified pieces. In order to make a psychological mosaic, one must first recognize the fragments. Recognition of traumatic fragments can be a challenge, as they are rarely addressed. In life, they alter the ability to sustain relationships,

KEY PIECES

> A mosaic redefines the purpose and use of pieces to create a new whole.

> The fragments of trauma penetrate life, leaving people stricken when resolution is not found.

> Reformulation poetry creates a mosaic from the language of traumatic wounds.

jobs, goals, dreams, and live healthily.[1] Creating a mosaic from psychologically embedded fragments is a way to reform trauma in the present with a new meaning. Mosaics of trauma use the shattered pieces of self, caused by an unaddressed traumatic event, to reconstruct meaning in the present, thereby helping one to move beyond a state of crisis. The images of the events must be understood in order to create a mosaic that responds to the trauma. In the first chapter of *Testimony: Crisis of Witnessing in Literature, Psychoanalysis, and History*, by Shoshana Felman and Dori Laub, Felman writes, "to seek reality is both to set out [and] to explore the injury inflicted by it - to turn back on, and to try to penetrate, the state of being stricken, [and] wounded by reality ... ".[2] To recognize the fragments of trauma one must return to an injured state, and explore each shattered piece through the injury. The effort is emotionally distressing and may leave an individual in a state where the trauma persists in the psyche and repeats through actions, words, and thoughts, when not addressed. This feeling may leave an individual buried beneath heaps of broken images. A mosaic response can be found in reformulation poetry. By reformulating the language of wounds, through collaborative poetry, one can use broken images to make a mosaic which permits an individual a reformulation of the earlier and compiled traumas in their subconscious.

THIS DOES NOT ELIMINATE THE TRAUMAS OR RID THEM FROM THE INDIVIDUALS THAT HAVE REFORMULATED THEM; IT WORKS AS A METHODOLOGY THAT ALLOWS A CREATION OF SOMETHING NEW IN THE SUBCONSCIOUS, ESSENTIALLY ALLOWING THE INDIVIDUAL TO SEE FLECKS OF PAST TRAUMAS PERMEATE THROUGH THE NEW MOSAIC, BUT AS SOMETHING DIVERGENT AND REFORMED.

This process requires both a witnessing and a response. Writing poetry allows individuals to give traumatic testimony and to face their wounds by giving them a voice in seeking reality; additionally, reformulation poetry requires collaborative pairing. It stands on the premise of partners both giving testimony and bearing witness to one another's traumas. There is a freedom in this form of expression, and

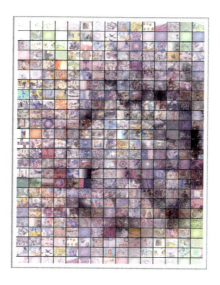

an equality of vulnerability. From that space of vulnerability, from the wounds of the traumas of each individual, and from the witnessing of each individual's address, a reformulated response can be made, a mosaic is created and a new meaning is defined.

THE FOUNDATIONS OF REFORMULATION POETRY

The basis for the theory of reformulation poetry lies in three factors. The first factor is a connection to literary trauma theory with a focus on examining literary works for aspects of trauma that may have otherwise remained hidden. The second factor is a close reflection of the crying wound in Cathy Caruth's book *Unclaimed Experience: Trauma, Narrative, and History*, which states that lives are shaped by past traumatic events that are ongoing and repeated in the present. The third factor is an examination of giving testimony, witnessing, and making an address from Shoshana Felman and Dori Laub's book *Testimony: Crises of Witnessing in Literature, Psychoanalysis, and History*, which states that acts that produce statements about traumatic

> *KEY PIECES*
> > Basis of Reformulation Poetry:
>   1. Literary Trauma Theory
>   2. The Crying Wound
>   3. Testimony, Witnessing, and making an Address.
>
> > The process of hearing the crying wound and making an address, by way of giving testimony to a witness and receiving a response, is a systematic approach to finding meaning.

events create an opportunity to be heard fully and responded to in ways that can help find meaning.

LITERARY TRAUMA THEORY

*E*xamining written works through the lens of trauma builds a world in which one may analyze both the conscious and subconscious scenarios. Spoken language holds the power of clarity, articulation, and reciprocation of thoughts; written language allows an individual access to self in a way that goes beyond thought and speech. The physicality of trauma can become a written artifact which can be viewed, read aloud and heard, or reflected upon in a way that the transience of speech prohibits.

KEY PIECES
> The physicality of trauma can become a written artifact.
> Artifacts of poetic writing are composed of emotion and metaphor; they are contemplative and psychologically rooted.
> A written poetic artifact of trauma is used as the foundation for reformulation poetry.

IN LITERARY TRAUMA THEORY, ARTIFACTS ARE READ THROUGH THE PSYCHOANALYTICAL LENS OF IDENTIFYING AND UNDERSTANDING TRAUMAS HIDDEN WITHIN THE LANGUAGE, UNWRITTEN ELEMENTS, TROPES, AND METAPHORS. IN REFORMULATION POETRY, METAPHORS ARE A NECESSARY TOOL TO GIVE TESTIMONY, BEAR WITNESS, AND FORMULATE A RESPONSE.

Writing poetry adds additional dimensions, it fosters a different type of encoding in the memory in its form of expression. It is contemplative, rooted, and can draw out thoughts that normally remain hidden. In *Testimony*, Felman writes,

> To seek reality through language 'with one's very being,' to seek in language what the language had precisely to *pass through*, is thus to make of one's own 'shelterlessness'- of the openness and the accessibility of one's own wounds - an unexpected and unprecedented means of *accessing reality*, the radical condition for a wrenching exploration of the testimonial function, and the testimonial power, of the language: it is to give reality one's own vulnerability, as a condition of exceptional availability and of exceptionally sensitized, tuned in attention to the *relation between language and events.*[1]

Writing transcends and bridges broken images, it gives way to vulnerability. Vulnerability in one's own reality is a realization of the permeance that the initial penetrating force was able to deliver. Thus the permeance of the wound weaves itself into an availability and a lack of defensiveness.

THROUGH THE WRITING PROCESS, ONE IS ABLE TO DRAW OUT TESTIMONIAL POWER AND MAKE SENSE OF TRAUMATIC EXPERIENCES, WHETHER THE EXPRESSION OF WHAT IS WRITTEN IS A DIRECT OR INDIRECT ARTICULATION.

When an event is voiced, a form of poetic storytelling is employed and the selected words expose the memory and emotions of the fragmented story. Each expressed micro-moment is used to weave the traumatic memory into a narrative. Portions of memory are avoided or forgotten and reverberate in their resounding silence and continued emotional weight. In *Unclaimed Experience*, Caruth writes of the necessity for a " ... new mode of reading and of listening that both the language of trauma, and the silence of its mute repetition of suffering, profoundly and imperatively demand".[2] One example that illustrates this mode is in *Testimony*, where Felman explores the process of writing recollections of dreams of trauma through examination of the "Irma dream" in Sigmund Freud's *Interpretation of Dreams*. Dreams have been widely studied and are at best nebulously understood; nonetheless, one outcome from a recalled dream is the articulation of a story and a series of images that are pronounced. Trauma can be presented as symbols or directly manifest as events and emotions in dreams. Expressed trauma accesses unbridled thoughts, feelings, and the human subconscious.

Felman writes,

> Through the material process of the act of *writing down* (which in some ways implicates the relevance, and the participation, in the psychoanalytic testimonial process, of the *literary act*): through a detailed recording and deciphering of the dream's associations ... *bears witness* to the *unconscious* testimony of the dream in such a way as to transform it into the most reflective and most pointed *conscious* testimony, a conscious testimony which itself can be only grasped in the movement of its own production, and which increasingly embraces not just what is *witnessed*, but what is *begotten* by the unconscious testimony of the dream.[3]

Dreams are a form of story and personal testimony. An attempt to decipher a dream, through the telling of it, is an attempt to access meaning. Dream journals and free association writing are often employed as a way to create an artifact of understanding. Writing is a fundamental technique in both testimony and witnessing of a dream. Similarly, writing poetry outside of a dream state carries with it an ability to access the testimony of trauma. The imagery of awakened written metaphors can free individuals from constraints of formality in language and structure. Poetry connects emotionally to an event at conscious and subconscious levels and can give articulation to the wounds of trauma as an artifact that can be reformulated. Felman's examination also supports the power of poetry, speaking to its ability to testify beyond its traditional means in her reflection of Stéphane Mallarmé:

> The very principle of poetic insight and the very core of the event of poetry, which makes precisely language - through its breathless gasps - speak ahead of knowledge and awareness and break through the limits of its own conscious understanding. By its very innovative definition, poetry will henceforth speak *beyond its means*, to testify - precociously - to the ill-understood effects and to the impact of an accident whose origin cannot precisely be located but whose repercussions, in their very uncontrollable and unanticipated nature, still continue to evolve, even in the very process of testimony.[4]

Poetic essence accesses the breathless gasps of an event; in the evolution of these unanticipated gasps, a wound is heard and can be accessed.

THE CRYING WOUND

A mental wound inflicted by a traumatic experience is synonymous, in ways, to a physical wound. However, where physical wounds are tangibly addressed through regeneration and are aided by physical therapies, an address of a mental wound requires a complex understanding of an intangible cry. In *Unclaimed Experience*, Caruth expands upon Freud's

> **KEY PIECES**
> > The crying wound captures the essence of how mental trauma reappears and returns continuously in a way that demands to be articulated and witnessed.
> > Traumatic memories do not translate into a narrative state; they persist as crying wounds.

XL

This found he graven in the tender rind,
And while he mused on this uncouth writ,
Him thought he heard the softly whistling wind
His blasts amid the leaves and branches knit
And frame a sound like speech of human kind,
But full of sorrow grief and woe was it,
Whereby his gentle thoughts all filled were
With pity, sadness, grief, compassion, fear.

XLI

He drew his sword at last, and gave the tree
A mighty blow, that made a gaping wound,
Out of the rift red streams he trickling see
That all bebled the verdant plain around,
His hair start up, yet once again stroke he,
He nould give over till the end he found
Of this adventure, when with plaint and moan,
As from some hollow grave, he heard one groan.

- Torquato Tasso | Gerusalemme Liberata

interpretation of the romantic epic poem of *Gerusalemme Liberata* by Torquato Tasso, stating that a wound cries out for acknowledgment. In the poem, Tancred unintentionally slays Clorinda, his beloved, who is disguised as an opposing knight. He then enters a forbidden forest where unbeknownst to him, Clorinda's soul has been imprisoned in a tree. Overcome with emotion, he stabs at the tree, and, out of the "wound", the voice of his love is heard.[1] Caruth writes,

> The actions of Tancred, wounding his beloved in a battle and then, unknowingly, seemingly by chance, wounding her again, evocatively represent in Freud's text the way that the experience of a trauma repeats itself, exactly and unremittingly, through the unknowing acts of the survivor and against his very will. As Tasso's story dramatizes it, the repetition at the heart of catastrophe— the experience that Freud will call 'traumatic neurosis'—emerges as the unwitting reenactment of an event that one cannot simply leave behind.[2]

This thought captures the essence of a traumatic mental wound, against one's will the trauma repeats through unknowing acts. The initial penetrating event then reappears, seemingly without reason, and returns continuously throughout an individual's life; there is an inability to articulate the immensity of the wound. In this reappearance, the cry of the wound is a whispering scream, for it is repeatedly punctured by the subconscious. Caruth states that there is a voice that "is paradoxically released through the wound".[3] Once this scream is heard, the rush of emotion is perplexing and layered. It is compiled of the personal and collective traumatic events that have built up to that moment of recognition, and the weight is immense. When the scream is heard for the first time, the shame, sorrow, embarrassment, and fear reverberate within the listener, as the wound is exposed. Each original trauma poem in this book is representative of that voice. Tancred was not aware that he had been inflicted with an inner wound, he killed Clorinda, and he only knew of her death after he "killed" her a second time.

The puncturing of the original unknown wound is representative of how traumatic memories are encoded and recalled. Traumatic memory is initially encoded in dissociated fragments of sensations and emotional states that are not immediately transcribed into personal narratives as ordinary memories are. One study that took place, over a period of fifteen years, illustrated that individuals who had post-traumatic nightmares claimed they experienced unmodified traumatic recollection.[4] Essentially, traumatic memories do not transition into narrative states; these memories persist as crying wounds, triggered uncontrollably in the forms of dreams, hallucinations, and other intrusions that recall the trauma literally and vividly. It is in hearing the wound's scream that Tancred knew that it existed. The wound screams because it is demanding to be witnessed; there is a need for it to be free of its perpetual amberized state. It cries out because it wants the truth to be told, and for the original trauma to be exposed. Tancred freeing the scream of Clorinda is akin to freeing oneself from the repetitive continuous puncturing that trauma imposes on an individual. In *Testimony*, Shoshana Felman writes,

> To attempt ... to reemerge from the paralysis of [trauma], to engage reality [Wirklichkeit suchend] as an advent, a movement, [is] a vital, critical necessity of moving on. It is beyond the shock of being stricken, but nonetheless within the wound and from within the woundedness of the event, incomprehensible though it may be, becomes accessible. The wound gives access to the darkness which the language had to go through and traverse in the very process of its "frightful falling-mute".[5]

It is through the repetitive puncturing of the wound that the muted fragmented language of trauma becomes accessible; the silent scream is heard through the darkness and can be witnessed. In reformulation poetry, the scream can be witnessed in the form of a testimonial poem.

TESTIMONIAL POETRY

The testimonial poetic process works to expose the subconscious, specifically subconscious moments of trauma that are sealed up tightly within, what one could see as, mental crypts. While crypts are known to house the dead, these mental crypts house the remnants of events that were alive in their terror and sit waiting for resurrection; when opened the wound inside cries.[1] One does not necessarily choose a particular past traumatic event in which to write in this testimonial process. As one first starts to recollect fragmented memories, a visual disorientation of multiple layered images may appear. Confusion is a normal effect, triggered from the moment the trauma occurred; the interwoven fragments are threaded throughout the life of the individual and are present during memory recall. One image will stand out, that one image is the one that will repetitively puncture the fragments. This is the event the testifier must hone in on. In essence, the event chooses them, as its need to be free is intensified by traumatic recollection and repetition in the person's everyday life. Testimony is a resurrecting of the subconscious trauma into a poem,

> *KEY PIECES*
> > A mental crypt is the place where a traumatic event is encoded in the psyche of an individual.
> > One may not choose which traumatic fragments are recalled while opening mental crypts; however, if a trauma cries out, one must hone in on it.
> > Written testimonial poetry creates a safe space of respect which fosters a necessary witnessing and allows for the truth to be uncovered.

and through the act of writing the crypt is accessed. Writing out a recollection of an event through poetry will expose the testifier to the cries of a wound, and the event may seem questionable and unclear.

> ONE MUST NOT QUESTION THE AUTHENTICITY OF THE MEMORY, AS THE MIND WILL BRING TO THE FOREFRONT WHAT IT NEEDS IN ORDER TO RETRIEVE AN EVENT THAT HAD CAUSED SIGNIFICANT TRAUMA.

The retrieval process employs narrative memory, as the wound is exposed through its semantic and symbolic representation in the writing of a poem.[2] Testimony through poetry may not be a literal remembrance of the event that has occurred in its entirety. It may be a flash of memory, a face, or an event, and the individual may even question the validity of the memory, but the remembrance carries valid encoded emotion. The wound cries out to be heard whether the individual is able to understand what is occurring or not. In *Testimony*, Felman writes,

> As a relation to events, testimony seems to be composed of bits and pieces of memory that has been overwhelmed by occurrences that have not settled into understanding or remembrance, acts that cannot be constructed as knowledge nor assimilated into full cognition, events in excess of our frames of reference.[3]

Poetic recollection is an endeavor to fill in the blank spaces of consciousness with a reconstruction of images that one may have encountered through distortion in dreams, daily moments of misunderstanding, or flashbacks. When initiating the process of testimonial poetry, the memory tries to make sense of the jumbled pictures and events that are heaped inaccessibly; it works to fill in the blank space with imperfect flashes of memory and tries to penetrate the impenetrable. Poetry is the vehicle of testimony that fosters this penetration. Its creation is an act that gives access to the subconscious and conscious effects of allowing oneself to be vulnerable. Felman continues, "The testimony will thereby be understood, in other words, not as a mode of *statement of*, but rather as a mode of *access to*, that truth".[4] Written testimonial poetry creates a safe space of respect, which fosters a necessary witnessing and allows for the truth to be uncovered.

WITNESSING & AN ADDRESS

When one completes a testimonial poem there is an inherent desire and necessity to allow the testimony to be witnessed. In *Unclaimed Experience*, Caruth suggests that when listening to the cry of trauma, one must not only listen to what is being directly said, but what is being omitted.[1] She refers to this as "how to listen to the departure".[2] In order for a witness to hear the scream and search for an understanding of the underlying trauma, they must look for the departure in the narrative of the poem.

> **KEY PIECES**
> - A witness is an individual that can hear and respond to a testimony of trauma.
> - Witnessing must evoke empathy and an openness that is necessary to form a response. If these conditions are not met, an individual may not hear the wound and will be a false witness.
> - The response of an address requires authentic hearing and vulnerability.

THE DEPARTURE IS FOUND WITHIN THE BREATHLESS GASPS OF WHAT IS ABSENT IN THE WRITING AND IN THE RAWNESS OF AN UNSTRUCTURED CRY. ENTRANCE INTO THE WHISPER, BENEATH THE SCREAM OF THE WOUND, IS AN ENTRANCE INTO A SPACE OF VULNERABILITY WHICH THE LISTENER MUST ALLOW TO PERMEATE THROUGH THEIR BEING. THE LISTENER MUST EMBRACE THE VULNERABILITY OF THE TESTIFIER WITHOUT JUDGEMENT. WITNESSING MUST EVOKE EMPATHY AND AN OPENNESS THAT IS NECESSARY TO FORM A RESPONSE.

If these conditions are not met, the witness may not hear the wound and will become a false witness, incapable of forming a necessary response. False witnessing is voyeuristic, the witness subsumes the testifier's trauma to meet an internal desire to be a witness, to express one's sympathy rather than feel true empathy. It is dangerous to a be a false witness; if a false response is made, the wound will remain exposed.[3] Both the testimony and the witnessing must be authentic to see the wound from the event that occurred from a "rhetoric, semantic, phonemic, cryptonymic, and symbolic" perspective.[4]

When witnessing is authentic, the emotion of the testifier's trauma can permeate through the witness and needs to be identified, responded to, and addressed. When a permeation is not addressed, it can penetrate the witnesses psyche. For example, in *Testimony*, Felman wrote that she exposed her undergrad class to a two-part screening of a Holocaust film in which a woman spoke of her tragic experiences. She wrote that students looked subdued as they first viewed the film and that the class had ended in silence; however, the silence of what was witnessed did not carry forward outside of the class. In the weeks to come, students repetitively spoke about the film to one another, any others that would listen, and called Felman outside of work hours. They felt a sense of fragmentation, disconnect, and described the experience as shattering. Felman felt that she had a duty to help her class be free of the trauma that was permeating within their state of being. Prior to beginning the second part screening, she chose to address the students fragmentation by summarizing what occurred in the first viewing using their own words and then followed with a review of the class readings and corresponding videos from the first part screening. She contextualized a prior reading of Paul Celan's Holocaust experience with the classes own experience. As witnesses, her students had absorbed the wound of another; they felt helpless to resolve this permeation. Felman identified and addressed the permeation of the wound, finally inviting the class to write a paper of testimony of their experience which helped them find their role as the witness within the fragmented disconnect.[5]

The process of reformulation poetry reflects risks of witnessing that are similar to the initial outcomes in Felman's class. In reformulation poetry, there is collaborative witnessing. Each testifier is also a witness, and this double witnessing may have complex repercussions. Normally, the witness bears "the solitude of the responsibility, and to bear the responsibility, precisely of that solitude".[6] Reformulation poetry moves beyond solitude in the act of witnessing and responding to trauma because two people engage in the space of vulnerability through partnership. This is necessary to avoid an outcome of fragmented paralysis in collaborative witnessing. In *Unclaimed Experience,* Caruth writes, "an address of voice … [is] the "story of the way in which one's own trauma is tied up with the trauma of another".[7] She continues, " … listening to the address of another … [is] an address that remains enigmatic yet demands a listening and a response".[8]

> THE TESTIMONY GIVEN AND THE PRESENCE OF A WITNESS IS NECESSARY TO ALLOW BOTH INDIVIDUALS SPACE TO UNDERSTAND HOW THEIR STORIES OF TRAUMA ARE STORIES THAT BOND THEM. THIS BOND FACILITATES CRUCIAL SPACE; SPACE FOR VULNERABILITY, SPACE TO HEAR THE VOICE OF THE WOUND, AND SPACE TO FORMULATE A RESPONSE BORN OF UNITY.

In *The Waste Land* Eliot wrote,

> For you know only a
> A heap of broken images, where the sun beats,
> And the dead tree gives no shelter, the cricket no relief,
> And the dry stone no sound of water. Only
> There is shadow under this red rock,
> (Come in under the shadow of this red rock)[9]

While the poem itself has an overarching feeling of desolation, an address creates a space to erase the solitude between the person giving testimony and their witness by way of invitation. Eliot beckons to

Clorinda to look towards " ... the shadow of this red rock".[10] In reformulation, the red rock is turned over and exposes the poetry of testimony; the witnessing illuminates the shadows. It is through this bond that the person who gives testimony and the person who bears witness create a crucial sense of trust that is necessary to take on the act of reformulation. The witness is the first to formulate the words of response, but this can only happen after listening to the voice of the wound.

TO FACILITATE LISTENING, A WOUND EXPRESSED THROUGH POETRY MUST BE READ ALOUD.

By reading the trauma aloud as a poem, the person giving testimony allows the witness to hear the cry, to feel it course through them, and to understand the parts of the poem that are most difficult to express. Without the actual voice being heard, listening cannot occur. If a person bears false witness, a response cannot be formed, and the act of reformulation will be empty. Upon reading a reformulated poem created by a false response, the traumas from the shared testimonies will not find new meaning and remain open wounds. The language of the wounds must be reformulated directly into a mosaic artifact. This can only be done when the act of witnessing is authentic and each individual feels the other's wound as well as their own wound. A newly reformulated poem is viewed as a response of both witnesses to the fragmentation of the wounds.

REFORMULATION

*T*o witness is to untangle layered and heaped fragments, and in a way, each individual becomes a cryptographer. By combining personal traumas, collaborators receive the compassion of each other's traumas intertwined, allowing them to bond through the reverberation of the wound and to break the code of the trauma. In reformulation poetry, both individuals give written testimony simultaneously; by creating their poems of trauma together, they each puncture their wounds, knowing their collaborator is doing the same. The scream of each wound is shared in a space of vulnerability. By facing, hearing, and feeling each scream, an individual recognizes the broken images of the other's scream amalgamating with their own.

> **KEY PIECES**
>
> \> Reformulation is the process by which two partners simultaneously give testimony, bear witness to one another's traumas, and respond through collaborative reconstruction and redefinition of the initial poems of trauma.

FEELINGS OF IMMENSE GUILT, SHAME, AND EXPOSURE SEEM TO COME FROM THE PUNCTURING OF THE WOUND, AND THUS A SPACE OF VULNERABILITY IS CRUCIAL.

Reformulation poetry is the creation of a mosaic from both wounds within this vulnerability; in expanding on the language of *The Waste Land*, it is the intertwining of tree branches outstretched across the space of two red rocks, reaching above the shadows into the light and making it into a mosaic. In the act of creation, the voice of the response can be heard with a new strength. The broken images are used to create a completely new image in which there is redefined meaning. A response has been made to each trauma. It has been written and can be referenced, it can be understood and reexamined, and it has forever been encoded into the memory of the wounded individual, changing the voice that cried.

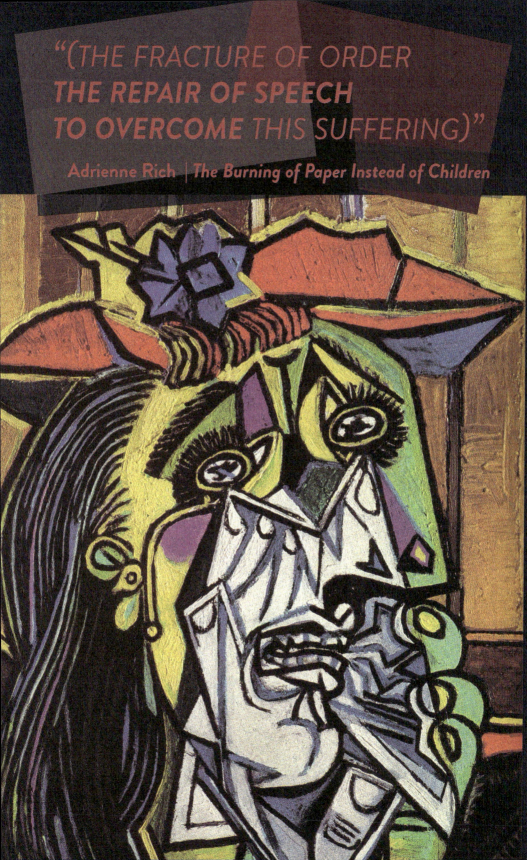

> "(THE FRACTURE OF ORDER
> THE REPAIR OF SPEECH
> TO OVERCOME THIS SUFFERING)"
>
> Adrienne Rich | *The Burning of Paper Instead of Children*

The Reformulation Process
How to Create a Mosaic

THE PROCESS

To create a mosaic, a reformulated poem of new meaning, two individuals must first partner and then collaborate.

> THE PARTNERSHIP MUST BE ONE THAT FACILITATES VULNERABILITY.

Each individual will access memories of a trauma and will share its scream; to do so requires space and trust in the partnership. The space must be free of judgement or expectation, it must feel safe. To give testimony in an unsafe environment can lead to outcomes where the cry of the wound is not fully heard on an individual level and is therefore captured in a disjointed or constrained testimony. By accessing a crying wound and giving testimony, witnessing can occur. Both individuals can make an address and prepare to respond to the entwined crying of their wounds together. Vulnerability and trust can be created between partners through two key principles: a willingness to be open to the process and to oneself, and the understanding that giving testimony is a reciprocal event that leads to an act of creation through collaboration. In the simultaneous exposure of each individual, judgement and fear of rejection can be held at bay.

REFORMULATION POETRY

1. **Preparing Yourself**

   You will need at least a two hour time period with your partner to reflect and write. Accessing wounds of trauma is difficult.

   YOU WILL GIVE TESTIMONY TO A TRAUMA THAT CRIES OUT WITHIN YOU, AND THE EXPERIENCE CAN BE DISORIENTING AND EMOTIONALLY EXPOSING; THIS IS IMPERATIVE TO UNDERSTAND.

   Your partner will also be giving testimony to a trauma. Remember that you are in a space without judgement, no matter what is voiced, and will want to be in a physical environment where each of you feels safe.

2. **Accessing a Crying Wound**

   Both you and your partner will start by silently reflecting and allowing your mind to enter the space of memories where you have felt hurt. You will recall an image, voice, smell, or another type of fragment of an event. This may lead to thoughts of other unrelated fragments of traumas, but one image will stand out repetitively. Focus on that image, allow yourself to recall any associated memories and emotions that come with it.

3. **Writing a Poem of Testimony**

Each of you will take personal time to write a poem without restraint of any poetic formality. You could be a master of poetry or could have never written a poem before. The idea of writing a poem may even seem awkward or intimidating; it is important to remember that the poem is not being judged on aesthetic qualities or at any other level. It is not necessary to make it rhyme or have rhythm, but if these elements come naturally let your writing go where it needs to. It is through the act of writing, through the act of accessing the language of the wound's cry, that the poem is born, and it will take on whatever form it needs to. By writing in this way, the wound's cry will be authentic. When you feel ready, begin writing a poem of your crying wound.

EXAMPLES OF POEMS OF TESTIMONY

> Humanity at its worst
> Heritage shattered
> Culture a shambles
> Life so ephemeral
> We transition through space + time
> with some luck
> So many others with less fortune
> In the wrong place at the wrong time
> Victims of an identity card
> with the wrong identity
> Occupation. Desecration. Dehumanization
> Still ongoing for so many more
> Why do we go on oblivious to their pain?

A WARM DAY IN SUMMER

The wind is warm
The air is sweet
I feel the warmth of my father's love
He holds me, he plays with me
He teaches me to pronounce my "R's"
I jump in his lap, he nuzzles me with a kiss

Then he turns one day to become cold
He expects, he rejects, he demands
His disposition turns cold
Like the chilly wind of fall

What have I done?
Why has this changed?
I'm alone on the outside
I'm being run over
I'm under attack, just a small boy
Alone, lost, detached

I push the row boat into the water
I row out farther and farther from shore
I don't know where to go except away, away
What to do? I don't want to go back
I want to go out, away, away
I don't want to go back to the cabin

I sitee at the floor boards of my boat
The sun shines down on my back on my firm skin
I know I have come to a point of no return
Either he runs over me or I stand up to him
He is now the face of evil
My dear father the person I must NOW stand unto
This change everything....

I decided to stand up
To not be run over
But what I lost....

There is no path before me,
With this boy,
I am the boy,
Oh boy

In the innocence of you
Yout
Youth I mean
I f-f-feeel

I feel I feel
Don't put that toy
Near me,
You want, need what?

Where?
No, no
But I look up
And I see you
Like a powerful sun

Like a spirit guide
What spirit guide
Pen

Me?

I suppose this is the way
Things are this way
I am this way
Am I this way?

I will eat the peach
And continue forward
Blind
No longer blind

In the light of of of of

This.

Pinpoint the pen.
An immaculate plan sets forth.
Riding on the broken back of digested lore,
And phantoms of old family secrets.
An imprint stamped on innocent flesh.

Go away old man with crippled hands,
You loom to close.

Unwelcomed whimsical terror
Incites my throne.
And all around the water people shout, retreat!
The forest holds the dreams of now
And a path that twists around that house,
Where I know not the occupant.

I remember that car that took me,
For a chocolate bar.

I let you make a world by mine,
And yours was filled with carnage.
I left that magical barrier made of bubbles.
Thankfully my world was only slightly singed.

4. **Privately Reading Your Poem of Testimony**

    Once the two poems are written, each of you will privately read your own poem and you will pause for reflection on the wound that is exposed and captured on paper. The initial release of the wound onto paper can feel cathartic, frightening, painful, induce shyness, or trigger a range of other emotions. It is important to remember that each of you will experience this initial exposure in a personal way and to be mindful of the partnership. No matter the emotion conveyed or hidden, you must look at one another without judgement. For example, in the act of writing and reflecting either of you may show signs of emotional distress. Address one another with compassion if these moments occur.

5. **Sharing and Witnessing the Poems of Testimony**

    Once you have each read your poem of testimony privately, the collaborative sharing process begins. Both of you will share your poem verbally. Reading aloud makes the voice of the wound audible. The person listening, the witness, should first hear the scream of the voice, hear what is conveyed, and should pause their mind to see and understand what the voice of the wound is saying. It is in this pause, that the departure in the narrative can reverberate and can be heard, and an understanding of the wound is found. A reflective discussion may be necessary afterward to facilitate understanding. When both testimonies are witnessed, a response can then be formed through collaboration.

6. Deconstructing the Poems of Testimony

When both testimonies are witnessed, the reformulation process can begin. To start, you will both collaborate to break apart the poems into stanzas or lines. Further deconstruction may be necessary as the reformulated poem is created, you may need to cut lines down to words, or words down to letters that can be combined to form new words. As the process of creation begins, the necessary level of deconstruction is revealed.

EXAMPLES OF DECONSTRUCTED POEMS

PERMEATE & PENETRATE

7. Creating a Reformulated Poem

Once the stanzas, lines, or words are in an elemental form, you can begin to reconstruct a reformulated poem with your partner. The poem is a response to the wounds that are rooted in each of you. The following example comes from two individuals who went through the process. It demonstrates a deconstruction of two stanzas of trauma and their reconstruction into a reformulated poem:

Testimony 1

Dirty in the dark
The two embark
Searching a time toward calm
They were a crew
They would follow through ...

Testimony 2

It was an instrument
Passed along to be played
Person after person
Strained to make a single note
Discordant sound
C ut s
A par t l v es
And I tried my turn ...

Reformulation

He is a tune
An instrument searching towards calm
He feels and knows the beat
I watch the Naked power embark
It twangs and I follow through the dark ...

In these particular poems of testimony, it was necessary for the partners to sometimes deconstruct words into letters. Those individual letters were then recombined into new words. The mosaic response in this example reflects an understanding of the traumas through an actively addressed, cognitive, and organized construct. As the poem continued, it responded to the pains articulated in the original wounds. For one testifier it allowed the wound to be seen, acknowledged, and to be free of judgement for the first time. For the other testifier, it forgave an inner monster that caused immense shame and disgust. Each wound required its own response in the reformulated poem. In this example, it was requisite to climb away from the state of being that the wound inhabited by freeing each testifier from their mental crypts.

8. **Reading the Reformulated Poem**

A KEY CONSIDERATION: In the process of creating a mosaic response, you and your partner will need to ensure that responses to the testimonies weave together to empower both of you. If one of you feels that the reformulation does not create a response to your address, then a reformulation has not fully occurred. The mosaic response will be incomplete. If the mosaic is an incomplete artifact, the process does not end. A wound that is exposed and does not have a response can be damaging to the psyche and will remain open.

After the reformulated poem is constructed, it should be read aloud. You can both read the poem, take turns, or just one of you can read, but the reformulation must have a voice to facilitate a

reclamation in the present. The voice allows the redefinition of wounds that are forever changed to be heard. When this voice is contemplated for the first time, a new strength will permeate into a change that will encode itself into the memory of each you. By collaboratively redefining two poems of trauma, a wound cannot be separated from the reformulated response and you can be free from the repetitive piercing cry that penetrated you.

IT IS IMPERATIVE TO CONTINUE REFORMULATING THE POEM PHYSICALLY UNTIL BOTH WOUNDS HAVE A VERBALLY RECOGNIZED AND RESONANT RESPONSE.

Testimonies & Reformulated Poems

TESTIMONY - REFORMULATION SET #1

TESTIMONY 1

It's the sink again,
That steady drip, drip, drip,
A leak from inside, somewhere
And no one knows why.

D on't you know that momentary maintenance is always
R equired? If the effort to repair is slack
I know that flooding comes, drudging up sludge
P utrid smelling, from the bowels of who knows where

D isgusting scum, and an assessment post mortem
R egression is the word of the day
I nsolence will not be tolerated.
P inkish tears turn hard, crystallizing into

D umbness.
R un run to the next person
I lluminate a single moment and
P erhaps I'll be saved.

It's the sink again,
That endless drip, drip, drip
Can someone cut the faucet already?

TESTIMONY 2

Water rush streams
Over thighs
A deep baptismal drowning
Blasphemy
Overt sexuality
Dusting the banisters
Of deception in a home
Filled with lies
Fight, flight,
Frozen
The dial is all sticky
Smell your fingers.
Fazing in and out
Starlight and sunbeams
Records in a sunstream
I'm awake

REFORMULATION

A Frozen leak knows Required maintenance.
cut the Putrid baptismal faucet out
Fazing next to Blasphemy streams.
all moments of know no, Come again?
It's that Illumination Always of
a sunstream crystallizing into Fight.

an assessment post mortem already is
Of the dialing effort, steady,
Dusting Over where you know,
Perhaps I'll be Overt?
know that A yearnless drip,
drudging up with Pinkish Insolence,
turns hard somewhere And someone lies. who?
I, A person, will Dash and tear and
flood Disgusting sticky scum in a Dumbness
drown The sludge in words of Starlight repair.
Run awake deep inside,
sink That drip, drip, drip, know
why, It's the fight again.

the banister is Regression's end
If That drip from the bowel is deception
then the knowing smells
the sink Water Filled the riptide run,
though not tolerated for a single moment.
in slack sand sexuality beacons
Your sunbeam Smells linger
I'm home today, saved.

TESTIMONY - REFORMULATION SET #2

TESTIMONY 1

Heavy and somewhat sweet air
Polish the rocks and sell them
Sold to the next highest bidder
For money of the mind
                requires only thoughts
Brown carpet
      large room
            small room
                  all rooms
Crooked gnarled fingers trace
Breast buds barely formed.
Pressure pinpoints the darkness
Ashamed of the excitement.
Chest to chest
Corpsified in unity
An inner unleashed howl
drops into a vault
Sealed and locked.

TESTIMONY 2

There is no path before me,
With this boy,
I am the boy,
Oh boy

In the innocence of you
Yout
Youth I mean
I f-f-feeel

I feel I feel
Don't put that toy
Near me,
You want, need what?

Where?
No, no
But I look up
And I see you
Like a powerful sun

Like a spirit guide
What spirit guide
Pen

Me?

I suppose this is the way
Things are this way
I am this way
Am I this way?

I will eat the peach
And continue forward
Blind
No longer blind

In the light of of of of
This.

REFORMULATION

Want,
Buds like a powerful sun
I feel the heavy and somewhat sweet air
Where with this boy things are this way
There is innocence of you
yout
Youth I mean   drops
I feel and I see you near me,
Like a spirit guide
I suppose I am barely this
Blind sold and corpsified bidder
What? No
Don't sell them
FIngers trace the mind
        Chest to Chest
Peach Breast next to you
An inner unleashed howl
I f-f-feeel
I am the light of of of of
This excitement
Oh boy
Eat
For that is the way of need
Put the highest path before me
And I will continue forward
What me? Ashamed of the
    small room
        large room
            brown carpet
                all rooms
            the boy
          money
        crooked gnarled toy ??
No, no

I look up into thoughts only
Sealed in pen
Polish the vault
But this way requires a spirit guide
Formed in the rocks
Pressure pinpoints the darkness
And locked in unity
I am this way
No longer blind

TESTIMONY - REFORMULATION SET #3

TESTIMONY 1

Pinpoint the pen.
An immaculate plan sets forth.
Riding on the broken back of digested lore,
And phantoms of old family secrets.
An imprint stamped on innocent flesh.

Go away old man with crippled hands,
You loom to close.

Unwelcomed whimsical terror
Incites my throne.
And all around the water people shout, retreat!
The forest holds the dreams of now
And a path that twists around that house,
Where I know not the occupant.

I remember that car that took me,
For a chocolate bar.

I let you make a world by mine,
And yours was filled with carnage.
I left that magical barrier made of bubbles.
Thankfully my world was only slightly singed.

TESTIMONY 2

The construct is immense
At first the aesthetic is enough
The pleasant boxes in a row
The hum of a system
Go, go and be
Under guise
No one will see
Slither weak, don't get stepped on
You might cry
O'almighty forbid!
The gold
The "betterment"
Temples of worship
Usurp my fuck
All imparted in daily ethics
"That's just not right."
What did you ever want?
No need to continue
There are boxes to live in if need be
I don't, never did
Let me be
Let it be
Let go
There is always tomorrow
And that's where I must be.

REFORMULATION

The gold hum of a magical world
Old And immense, fills my throne.
You make a world by mine
An immaculate plan sets forth.
The whimsical Temples need to continue
I welcome pleasant singed terror
that's where I must be.
There is always a path of bubbles
An imprint, ever better imparted
our daily Riding cry "to live, to be"
Left never to loom close. And Slither weak
See That's just not right ok
Usurp that ethics boxcar of The old family aesthetic
A mighty lore in "Let go and be!"
Let go and holds the dreams of now And that
Go For it
I know the occupant of My digestedment don't
around that was a man with one Fuck yo
remember that The forest lightly Incites flesh.
And phantoms And pen Angel people Let me Pinpoint YoU
Stamped guise constructs, broken worship crippled, all innocent
Twists the first with that, Under No thin barrier
I Forbid Owner barrages, Go away box systems That Are retreat, enough
Oh secret tomorrow What did you want of. me, Where will I be?
the water houses don't get a row
I Counted not my steeped sunshout! Thankful.
Nice on the last Falcon back of The mighty need
Dilated hocus is looped around yours
If The only one .can.be. in be made We

TESTIMONY - REFORMULATION SET #4

TESTIMONY 1

Dirty in the dark
The two embark
Searching a time toward calm
They were a crew
They would follow through
Going maliciously into the night
Brain fists and humiliation
Work happily towards obliteration
Naked parts were flickers of thoughts
Flash and watch
Watch and join
Be the parts you know.
Hold the power
Of this intimate hour
And roll over and rip off your clothes.
He knows, I think he knows
He most definitely feels and knows
Open your mouth feel the tune
Glossy friend of mine.

TESTIMONY 2

It was an instrument
Passed along to be played
Person after person
Strained to make a single note
Discordant sound
C ut s
A par t l v es
And I tried my turn

A mirror haunts the periphery
Even now, ap art i n t h e s p   ace
For shame for shame
In absolution the longing
Twangs, I want to say thank you
But how-
This dark ball is lodged
-In my knee
It hobbles me, that I could (ever be)

A picture viewed recently
The eyes are all tells
Guilt is a projection
And shackle, a collar
Society a hand, tugging
Apar t- I can't stand right now-
I beat the ground
Rhythm to feel, do you feel?
I know you do, but I need you to
Help cu t me more.

REFORMULATION

He is a tune
An instrument searching towards calm
He feels and knows the beat
I watch the Naked power embark
It twangs and I follow through the dark
In absolution and longing
Towards brain projection
The eyes open
Roll over
But they are all glossy
A picture viewed recently haunts the periphery
Of the flickers of thoughts
That Hold Dirty fists of tugging guilt and humiliation
This intimate hour tells how a time cut The two parts were discordant sound
For shame for shame
Person after person
Going maliciously into the night
A crew lodged
It most definitely hobbles ground
In society's clothes
Flash and watch and rip off your
Would
    Could
        Can't
Be the parts you know
The rhythm to
Feel
    Think
        Be
Do you feel a ever obliteration?
This dark ball shackle,collar were knee cuts
I know you do, but I need you to feel a single note happily
A part lives in the space
I want to say friend

I know
Mine was tried
Passed along
And even now apart
I stand right now-
A mirror
They join strained to make apart work
And turn to be played a hand - in my mouth
He know me more.
Help is me,
       my
            Your
Thank you

PERMEATE & PENETRATE

TESTIMONY - REFORMULATION SET #5

TESTIMONY 1

But for the innocence of youth
Again, young, again
Eyes shine love but the truth
Is something that must be rent:
Smiles all do wear
A promise at ease
Trust is leveraged with a swear
The rope that binds loose at first
Innocence in a noose, hurt
To the core of friendship
A need to prove
Has that feeling been removed?

Screaming words of spittle (silent)
Fear and confusion mix to create
A word with no language
Call it   , yes that
You see, I see, I don't see
Crystal o crystal tell me
In your shards
Hippocampal obfuscation
Is necessary, is it not?
A nudity present
Like a trussed up pheasant
Struggle to free
But the wolves descend.
Alone to be devoured
Memories scoured
And only a desire to let oblivion
Steal this one away.

TESTIMONY 2

A slight look
A crooked smile
Welcome to the street where no one-
that was anyone -
watched anyone -
That was anyone
They needed to watch.
Where parents smoked
And frogs were frozen in the dark.
Where the mean grew rapidly on the breath of little boys saying "take of your clothes"
And girls would run and fall
Just to be pounced on and fake escapes.
The pighoven man
Whistled
He whistled and watched.
A slight look
A crooked smile

REFORMULATION

for the innocence
little boys And girls would run to
Where the pheasant And frogs were
o crystal shards of youth
Again, free to be let away
this no the- A
the truth Is A crooked look I swear
But Memories promise, but
Innocence escapes To   .

Hippocampal Crystal tell me
Where was anyone that was with language?
no They needed to watch.
Call it anyone trussed up In oblivion
see, see:
Struggle on the breath
The rope that binds Trust
A net of
friendship- parents?

Smiles crooked, at ease in a noose
something must be Whistled
A Screaming mix
A slight obfuscation
A nudity present
all do wear clothes
A need to hurt that feeling
Fear and confusion create
A word.
words whistled and watched
fall loose at first
leveraged with a necessary desire
spittle Has been removed, devoured
to be Alone is to Steal a saying

"anyone that watched Is fake. take off your rented smile."
scoured, that smoked look is your-
yes I don't see that
But grow rapidly
Just to pounce on the only one of a.

Welcome to the street where You and I, slight and young again
descend Like wolves on The mean pighoven man
Eyes shine- smile frozen (silent) in the dark deed
And prove THE core of love.

START OF REFORMULATION

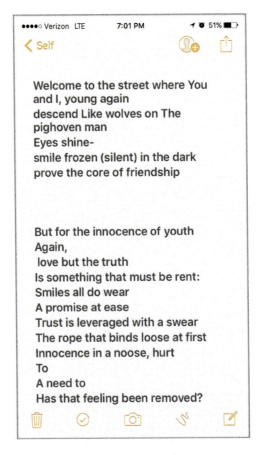

PERMEATE & PENETRATE

ORIGINAL POEMS BROKEN DOWN

NEARLY COMPLETE REFORMULATION

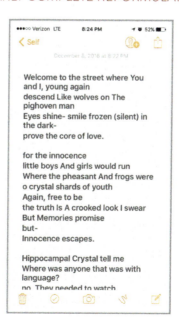

TESTIMONY - REFORMULATION SET #6

TESTIMONY 1

Porcelain, frantic
Little doll, crying in the night
Crying in glass eyed fright
Wanting so badly to be noticed
For more than my appearance
I cried for you,
  to do,
  to do
What you were supposed to.
You never did, I never knew
That you would never
Ever give me what I needed.
A distorted search to occupy the hole
I distorted figure to satisfy the goal
Broken doll
Unloved doll
Singing songs of innocence
Injected with broken bits of records
From the past
A happy little doll
A pretty little doll

TESTIMONY 2

The roars echo through the chambers
Of the bizarre funhouse
As I see it, mirrors reflect
A giant-
Can part the two callers
Calm them, will you please stop

Another day no more than a speck
A quivering helpless speck
What happens when trees fall?
The leaves come first, covering the ground
Where I reside
Where even smaller specks reside
Will we grow into the same shapes?

Shadows dance in the warped light
One leaves, one comes
One leaves
And another-
What these shadows are trying to say
Is little boys and girls should be

Cut apart the cord
The only threads left are
Discords, sly slips from bewitched tongues
Whence did the Anger Caster learn to win
So easily?

REFORMULATION

The roars echo through Where I reside
Injected with Shadows From the past
Trees dance in the night
And covering the ground I see happy leaves Singing songs.
Pretty Leaves Occupy the Porcelain glass shadows
Leaves Calm them,
search in the daylight or evening
my appearance mirrors the love
A doll- A little doll Wanting to fly
Will first Cut apart little threads of A distorted bizarre speck.
little boys and girls should reflect innocence
you did stop For no more than What you Were supposed to, bewitched
please help dress in all Fun-eyed tongues
I never knew That warped Whole,
nod to What would come
it resides for you the ever Be, you give me what I need
You figured, Ever trying the heart
Can a speck part the two Chambers?
no, doll callers notice the small house Is never the cord
These bits of records will grow into One another
Now, Can easily CUT Discords Of A badly crying broken speck doll fright
Whence the Little broken Anger slips from distorted cries
Where dying to say less happens to quiver,
learnt to be Doll no more As I did See
A giant door has come
we Are the same shapes, only he and I are left
win the goal to satisfy The One

TESTIMONY - REFORMULATION SET #7

TESTIMONY 1

The overlord of flawed actuality
Declares his Peripheral reality
It lays disturbed by filtered overtness
Visions clear and visions moist
Equally blurring to make pedestals
Smeared vaseline and black messes
Hot messes
Fucked flesh
Incoherent from the deepest prospect of
This gilded gold hunt of witches
Trust not them
Trust not they
What's in a pronoun?
Just a thousand years of fuck yourself.
It lays like a serpent coiling slowly
Asphyxiation is pleasure
Love it - For a time- love it
Invisibility cloak fastens on
Intelligence is sexy now
Wrap yourself in sexy intelligence
Lay on a hill and roll down it in childhood splendour

TESTIMONY 2

Addled brain knock knock
Reconcile a tumor
Found in falseness.
It threatens in separation
And grows in two spaces
The shape of poison
Spreading into snowflakes
Melts into a reservoir.
Slam with chemicals
A notion diabolical-
It becomes the dam that contains.

Repress depress
Silence and faith
In the moments of why
Lie untold questions
That stem from an ongoing
Engine of tedium
Fueled by red screams
From a broken mirror.

The only mirror that matters
Is the one that is whole.

REFORMULATION

The shape of gilded snowflakes
a thousand years filtered black.
Silence and faith Declare flawed actuality
visions thin and moist Melt into a reservoir
It threatens and It lays Smeared Peripheral reality a broken mirror

knock-
Trust not his overt falseness
it is a tumor of an Addled brain
                              -knock

The overlord of Hot vaseline messes
lays like a serpent coiling slowly
In moments of ongoing tedium
Repress depress why?
Asphyxiation is from red screams
And It fastens on a diabolical cloak
Spreading this hunt of gold witches
blurring love Just For a fuck
It grows into messes.

In Fucked flesh pedestals
untold questions of self
Wrap Incoherent poison chemicals
From within a tint
Invisibility spaces disturbed by separation
Reconcile notions That stem from Lies
Slam the dam that contains.

Trust your pronoun Love
Visions of yourself clear.
That matters.
Intelligence is The mirror to make the deepest Engine
sexy splendour Fueled by prospect

Lay on a hill and roll down it in pleasure.
Equally childhood becomes Found
intelligence is not the only sexy now
What time sense- them
in two Is the one that is whole.

START OF REFORMULATION

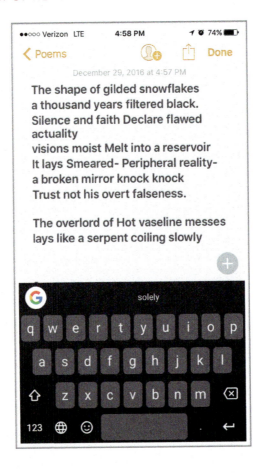

ORIGINAL POEMS BROKEN INTO PIECES

NEARLY COMPLETE REFORMULATION

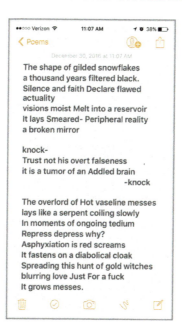

Interviews & Concluding Thoughts

INTERVIEWS

The following transcripts are the reflections of two partners that went through the process of reformulation poetry. The interview discusses their experiences going through the process. The identity of each individual has been anonymized to protect their privacy.

TESTIFIER 1

When you started the reformulation process, what did you think and feel?

Initially, I felt and was thinking about this slow drip from a faucet, and I do not know where that image came from, but it is one that has stayed with me for a long time. There is a phrase I heard once, about a pervasive tedium of life, that I tied to this dripping, this idea that I felt within me, where nothing I did would ever stop this drip. I do not know where that image came from, but all I saw was dirt, and the emotion of it was constant in strength and in a present pain that throbbed. But it was like a throbbing that was always there no matter what I did to try and shut it out, and sometimes it would feel acute, so all that ran through my mind.

Why did you enter into this process? Was it because of this throbbing? What was it that drew you to the idea of reformulation poetry?

When I heard about it, I felt a need to try. Try something. I have tried to get rid of and change this feeling, but it comes in spurts and there is imagery with it, I never understood why. Actually, I remember exactly why, I had written a short story that I had shared with my partner and we recognized that there was trauma in this short story, fucked up imagery, messed up imagery.

Can you explain how you initially met with the other collaborator, and how you felt?

The person I collaborated with was already my friend. I felt I needed someone I trusted a bit. We went over to a private space in a home. It was quiet, we sat on couches, and I remember feeling a bit apprehensive about sharing, and at the same time overcome with the ideas of the memories as they were already running through me. They were already there. I was already feeling a bit, of, the best word is uneasiness, but I wanted to stay open. I kept telling myself to stay open in my head.

Have you ever written poetry?

I have always enjoyed writing, but I have never officially published anything. If anything, my poetry was for myself, immature, and not studied formally.

What did you feel when you wrote your original poem? And what medium did you use?

Let me start by answering the medium question. I wrote on a computer, and I remember feeling, initially, a distance from myself. I could hear in my own mind a dripping, and the sound would get louder in my head and it turned to flooding, and there was a smell, like a putrid smell that turned into a flood; a smell, a dirty smell. I don't know what these images are from; I don't know what they are from. I felt really dark, captive to a darkness, and I was overcome. I felt vulnerable, and that I was a part of this darkness and disgusting. I also wasn't really comfortable writing the poem, so I think I imposed some structure because I was feeling out of control. So maybe I didn't fully let go, I don't know… something came out. The question I posed at the end, I felt like I was asking for help.

I noticed as we were talking about your original poem that you had an emotional response. Are you okay? Do you feel that the reformulation process did not help?

I mean, I feel some of the emotion as I recall this now. I don't feel overwhelmed if that makes sense? I don't feel a need to control, or stay quiet, or that I need help. There is still memory attached, a moment of remembering. The emotion I am feeling right now, is the emotion in that process [during the reformulation], but I don't hear the echoing drip, I can see the visual, but it's not there with all these questions. I don't look at it with fear or confusion. It doesn't matter in the same way. Since hearing the reformulated poem, I haven't once heard that drip again. I definitely feel that this helped. It is almost like an acceptance of whatever this memory is. I am actually rereading this poem, and I don't even know where some of this came from. I have a shitty memory though, this must be from my childhood, something that I somehow grabbed from somewhere. It was quiet or mute. I actually feel very disassociated now, I mean it doesn't feel like it was me, but it was me. Is that weird? It's weird. Now I feel shy.

Are you saying that the way that you respond now to the drip, or sound, is different from how you originally heard it? Was this sound of the drip something that followed you throughout your life?

Yes, I feel I have heard this sound accompanied with the idea that I would never fix it. Like a leaky faucet that would never be fixed. I felt helpless.

Do you feel helpless now?

No. I was crying for help, and I don't feel as if I need help now. Maybe more asking for help?

What was it like to hear another person's poem of trauma?

Well, initially my partner wrote and spoke and read a poem about water, and so, I felt that was in the first part. I remember that I felt connected through the water, I had the dripping faucet, a rush, and I felt that connection as I listened. In my mind, I tried to remind myself to be open and see the person, to just listen. I remember the poem was about a violation and it felt like it was during childhood, sexually. It included breakage of home and house, and then there was an element where the poem was talking to someone. I think it [the element] was to the person who had done the violation and I remember there was an idea of escaping into a more pleasant state of mind, but the end of the poem was the line " I am awake". I remember that. Let me tell you this right now, I can feel the poem of my partner, right now, actually. I feel this need to go back in time and stop it, which is ridiculous.

I don't feel it's ridiculous. I believe that you are just expressing the connection one feels when sharing something so intimate. What was the reformulation process like for you?

After my partner and I shared our poems, I felt very connected. I felt that they were as well. I had a sense of hopefulness and maybe some energy, there was this hurt and suffering that we shared from being heard. I couldn't stop from hearing that myself. I didn't feel unsafe or judged. Giving what they had shared, I only felt strongly for them. I felt that I heard them in every layer of who they are. When we went about breaking down the poems and then putting them back together, it seemed to fall in place. There were a lot of complementary words in the poems, such as smells, water, etc. When we were done it felt like we had put together something that was made of both of us, and then we read it aloud. I remember feeling like I heard what I needed to. I felt that in the process of creating the reformulated poem, and doing it with someone, I was being acknowledged. I felt that the poem helped me. I felt helped. But I will never forget this, I remember I read it aloud, my partner asked me to, and I looked up from reading it and saw their face and it was wracked with pain, the person's eyes. Looking straight into me, they said, "no, I still see it". I will never forget that; I will never forget that. I felt that in that moment, I had failed my partner. I felt that I just wanted to help them in the same way they helped me. We took a break and eventually tried again.

How long did the entire reformulation process take for you and your partner?

The whole process? It took about five hours because we had to do a second reformulation.

Can you talk about the second reformulated poem?

The second reformulation ... I think the main reason it took longer was because we were careful. I mean, when we were reading the first reformulation we realized it turned into something bigger. It almost seemed to augment the wound of my partner. It was like it took those words and made them more pronounced. In the second reformulation, we were more careful to be aware of removing the visibilities of that trauma.

When you chose to create a second reformulated poem, did your partner indicate that there were specific words that were problematic?

There were certain images in the poem that I could see were pronounced to begin with. Simply reusing them in a certain way, to redefine their meaning, was not enough. They needed to be addressed and responded to by removing them or changing them, by making new words.

Do you think that the feeling you had from the first reformulated poem, the feeling of being helped, carried with you into the second reformulated poem? Do you feel that the second reformulated poem helped your partner?

I felt, if anything, the second poem was more pronounced in the way it responded to my poem. The first one [reformulated poem] helped me by going through the act of bonding and creating because I was asking for help. I think the second poem did more to specifically change and redefine what happened, the trauma, the feeling of trauma; and my partner said they didn't see theirs [trauma] anymore. I knew, in that moment, it had helped both of us. We both had heard what we needed to.

TESTIFIER 2

When you started the reformulation process, what did you think and feel?

Let me just think about that. I guess that I felt there was a need to expel demons from myself, if that makes sense? Or it was something that's always been repeating in my brain over and over again, or some weird stuff that I know has negative connotations, and I'm a positive person, so I thought that this would be beneficial.

Have you written any poetry before?

Yes, I write poetry for fun sometimes. It was one of the reasons this was interesting to me, because I find poetry intriguing.

What did you feel when you wrote your original poem? And what medium did you use?

I used a computer and printed the poem after. It felt good entering into something that I thought may help me because I needed to dispel things that I wasn't happy with, that's kind of what I said earlier, but I was happy to do this, and it felt good to write stuff out. It actually wasn't until later, when I read it [aloud], that I felt bad about it. So reading it aloud was problematic, to me personally. Not writing, writing was fine.

Can you explain how you initially met with the other collaborator, and how you felt?

My partner and I are friends, and they mentioned this process, and I was in no way hesitant to do it. We ended up meeting, and it was very comfortable. I felt okay at the start of it, I felt ready to share. Reading my poem though? It was horrible. I didn't realize that reading poetry that you've written aloud is so exposing, and I don't like to be exposed, so it was challenging. I think our friendship, our relationship was helpful, specifically knowing what we were coming into, and understanding that we needed to be able to do this. I wasn't completely prepared for how I would feel when I read aloud, and I think my partner recognized that and was compassionate to it. I needed that [compassion], so yes, I think my partner helped me feel comfortable, and listened to, even though it was more than I expected [the feeling from reading aloud].

Do you feel your partner heard and understood what happened when you read aloud?

No, not initially, not in that moment. Writing it was the easy part and reading it was really hard, really fucking hard. I feel my partner saw or heard me, I felt that way, but in the reformulation part, I think it wasn't heard, if that makes any sense. There are intricacies in my writing that no one would know, moments of pain. Even when I was reading through my own poem, it was like flickers of images, so how would anyone know, if I don't? But I think it's because this person understood through their trauma, that I had some sort of trauma, that we connected in that way, but the intricacies were missed in the initial reformulation part.

Why do you feel the first reformulated poem didn't respond as you needed?

I clearly saw the circumstance that I was trying to get away from. I felt it was exposing me fully, and to read aloud to a person was humiliating. I didn't want to see that, and I felt powerless. It [the reformulated poem] wasn't broken down enough, that's what it came down to.

Did you want to try creating another reformulated poem afterward? What was different about the second reformulation? How do you feel now describing this experience to me?

Not initially, but I knew I needed to because I felt naked and vulnerable like I needed to put some clothes on. I didn't want to be exposed. I knew I had to continue on in the process because I saw merit in it. I saw that it helped my partner, and I didn't want to stay naked. The second reformulation took the most impactful words and moments and made them into beauty to me which is hard because the words are ugly. They made me feel ugly, and so to take what made me feel ugly and turn it into something different is very powerful. The second reformulation helped me. I feel overwhelmed with emotion, but good. I feel fine, and I actually like the line that has the worst words in it, which is weird, it is paired so well, so beautiful. It's like the one beautiful moment in that whole moment, there was one word that could actually be used for beauty, and it was. My partner thought, apparently, how things could go together, and I feel fine, I feel good, and I actually feel beauty, which is bizarre.

CLOSING THOUGHTS

When considering any one thing, there are questions. The questions stem from the relative inputs and outputs in being, in the object of consideration, in the person making the consideration, and in the relationship between them. Take, for example, a grain of sand; there are physical properties, metaphysical properties, symbolic properties, emotional properties, relational properties, unknown properties, and that is prior to adding in properties of interaction. A grain of sand is conceived of as a simple thing, but what then of designed miracle?

The possibility is absurd, the complexity is impenetrable, and the foundation for the existence of a miracle is unfathomable, let alone one created by design. And yet, what if? Is that hope? Does that absolve? What is truth?

NOTES

TRAUMA IN OUR CONTEMPORARY TIME

[1] "I. The Burial of the Dead" (2-4) by T.S. Eliot. Eliot, Thomas S. "The Waste Land": By T S Eliot. New York: Boni and Liveright, 1922. *Internet Archive*. Web. 22 Apr. 2017.

A TORRENT OF BROKEN IMAGES:
CONSTANT PENETRATION OF COLLECTIVE TRAUMAS

[1] Although the psychological impact was greatest among New York City residents (qtd. in Galea et al., 2002, 2003; Schlenger et al., 2002). (*Searching for and Finding Meaning in Collective Trauma* 1)

[2] In the days following the attacks, nearly half of Americans reported symptoms of posttraumatic stress (qtd. in PTS; Schuster et al., 2001). (*Searching for and Finding Meaning in Collective Trauma* 1)

[3] And many of these symptoms remained elevated in the following weeks and months (qtd. in Silver, Holman, McIntosh, Poulin, & Gil-Rivas, 2002). (*Searching for and Finding Meaning in Collective Trauma* 1)

[4] Even more common were fears of additional terrorist attacks, as more than half of Americans had ongoing concerns for the safety of themselves and their families (qtd. in Silver et al., 2002). (*Searching for and Finding Meaning in Collective Trauma* 1)

[5] Updegraff, John A., Roxane Cohen Silver, and E. Alison Holman. "Searching for and Finding Meaning in Collective Trauma: Results from a National Longitudinal Study of the 9/11 Terrorist Attacks." *Journal of Personality and Social Psychology* 95.3 (2008): 709-22. Print.

A MOSAIC RESPONSE

[1] In *Trauma and Recovery: The Aftermath of Violence - From Domestic Abuse to Political Terror*, Judith Herman writes,

> Traumatic events call into question basic human relationships. They breach the attachments of family, friendship, love, and community. They shatter the construction of the self that is formed and sustained in relation to others. They undermine the belief systems that give meaning to human experience. They violate the victim's faith in a natural or divine order and cast the victim into a state of existential crisis. (51)

Herman, Judith Lewis. *Trauma and Recovery: The Aftermath of Violence - from Domestic Abuse to Political Terror: With a New Epilogue by the Author.* New York: Basic, 2015. Print.

[2] On pg. 28 of "Education and Crisis, Or The Vicissitudes of Teaching" by Shoshana Felman in Felman, Shoshana, and Dori Laub. "1. Education and Crisis, Or The Vicissitudes of Teaching". *Testimony: Crises of Witnessing in Literature, Psychoanalysis, and History.* New York: Routledge, 1992. 1-56. Print.

THE FOUNDATIONS OF REFORMULATION POETRY:
LITERARY TRAUMA THEORY

[1] On pg. 28-29 of "Education and Crisis, Or The Vicissitudes of Teaching" by Shoshana Felman.

[2] On pg. 9 of *Unclaimed Experience: Trauma, Narrative, and History* by Cathy Caruth. Caruth, Cathy. *Unclaimed Experience: Trauma, Narrative, and History.* Baltimore: Johns Hopkins UP, 1996. Print.

[3] On pg. 16 of "Education and Crisis, Or The Vicissitudes of Teaching" by Shoshana Felman.

[4] On pg. 21-22 of "Education and Crisis, Or The Vicissitudes of Teaching" by Shoshana Felman.

THE FOUNDATIONS OF REFORMULATION POETRY:
THE CRYING WOUND

¹ Summarized from *Gerusalemme Liberata* by Tasso, Torquato. The image quotes stanzas XL-XLI from the Thirteenth Canto. *Gerusalemme Liberata ("Jerusalem Delivered")*. Translated by Edward Fairfax. London, 1600. Web. *Project Gutenberg*, http://www.gutenberg.org/ebooks/392.

² On pg. 2 of *Unclaimed Experience: Trauma, Narrative, and History* by Cathy Caruth.

³ On pg. 2 of *Unclaimed Experience: Trauma, Narrative, and History* by Cathy Caruth.

⁴ In *Dissociation and the Fragmentary Nature of Traumatic memories: Overview and Exploratory Study*, Bessel A. van der Kolk and Rita Fisler write,

> For example, in our own studies on post traumatic nightmares, subjects claimed that they saw the same traumatic scenes over and over again without modification over a fifteen year period (qtd. in van der Kolk, Blitz, Burr & Hartmann, 1984). (4)

Kolk, Bessel A., and Rita Fisler. "Dissociation and the Fragmentary Nature of Traumatic Memories: Overview and Exploratory Study." *Journal of Traumatic Stress* 8.4 (1995): 505-25. Print.

⁵ On pg. 28 of "Education and Crisis, Or The Vicissitudes of Teaching" by Shoshana Felman.

THE FOUNDATIONS OF REFORMULATION POETRY:
TESTIMONIAL POETRY

¹ On pg. 10 of "Fiction Begot Fiction: An Exploration of Trauma in William Faulkner's Novel The Sound and the Fury" by Terriann Walling. Walling, Terriann. "Fiction Begot Fiction: An Exploration of Trauma in William Faulkner's Novel The Sound and the Fury." *ECommons Home*. 01 Oct. 2012. Web. 23 Apr. 2017. https://ecommons.usask.ca/handle/10388/ETD-2012-10-592

[2] The semantic and symbolic properties of narrative memory are referenced from pg. 11 in "Table 2: Traumatic and Narrative Memory Compared" in *Dissociation and the Fragmentary Nature of Traumatic memories: Overview and Exploratory Study* by Bessel van der Kolk and Rita Fisler. On pg. 13 they continue,

> As the trauma came into consciousness with greater intensity, more sensory modalities came into awareness: initially the traumatic experiences were not condensed into a narrative. It appears that, as people become aware of more and more elements of the traumatic experience, they construct a narrative that "explains" what happened to them. This transcription of the intrusive sensory elements of the trauma into a personal narrative does not necessarily have a one-to-one correspondence with what actually happened. (13)

[3] On pg. 5 of "Education and Crisis, Or The Vicissitudes of Teaching" by Shoshana Felman.

[4] On pg. 16 of "Education and Crisis, Or The Vicissitudes of Teaching" by Shoshana Felman.

THE FOUNDATIONS OF REFORMULATION POETRY:
WITNESSING & AN ADDRESS

[1] On pg. 10 of "Fiction Begot Fiction: An Exploration of Trauma in William Faulkner's Novel The Sound and the Fury" by Terriann Walling. Walling, Terriann. "Fiction Begot Fiction: An Exploration of Trauma in William Faulkner's Novel The Sound and the Fury." *ECommons Home*. 01 Oct. 2012. Web. 23 Apr. 2017. https://ecommons.usask.ca/handle/10388/ETD-2012-10-592

[2] On pg. 10 of *Unclaimed Experience: Trauma, Narrative, and History* by Cathy Caruth.

[3] On pg. 39 of "An Interview with Robert Jay Lifton" by Cathy Caruth. Caruth, Cathy. "An Interview with Robert Jay Lifton." *Trauma: Explorations in Memory*. Baltimore: Johns Hopkins UP. 1995 Print.

[4] On pg. 7-8 of *Family Secrets and the Psychoanalysis of Narrative* by Esther Rashkin. Rashkin, Esther. *Family Secrets and the Psychoanalysis of Narrative*. Princeton, NJ: Princeton UP, 1992. Print.

[5] On pg. of "Education and Crisis, Or The Vicissitudes of Teaching" by Shoshana Felman.

[6] On pg. 3 of "Education and Crisis, Or The Vicissitudes of Teaching" by Shoshana Felman.

[7] On pg. 8 of *Unclaimed Experience: Trauma, Narrative, and History* by Cathy Caruth.

[8] On pg. 9 of *Unclaimed Experience: Trauma, Narrative, and History* by Cathy Caruth.

[9] "I. The Burial of the Dead" (21-26) by T.S. Eliot in *The Waste Land*.

[10] "I. The Burial of the Dead" (25) by T.S. Eliot in *The Waste Land*.

PHOTOS

Gerard, George - "Mosaic on Balboa." Digital Photo. 04 Apr. 2017. Web. 29 Apr. 2017.

Lehr, Lana. "Biography picture of Terriann." Facebook. 22 Jul. 2016. Web. 27 Feb. 2017.

NichoDesign. "Weeping Woman [1937]." Flickr. Yahoo!, 20 Nov. 2013. Web. 23 Apr. 2017. https://www.flickr.com/photos/nichodesign/10962390773

Qthomasbower. "Purple Flower - Fractal Mosaic." Flickr. Yahoo!, 22 Mar. 2009. Web. 27 Feb. 2017. https://www.flickr.com/photos/qthomasbower/3375798477.

QUOTES ON IMAGES

"I. The Burial of the Dead" (2-4) by T.S. Eliot. Eliot, Thomas S. "The Waste Land": By T S Eliot. New York: Boni and Liveright, 1922. Internet Archive. Web. 22 Apr. 2017.

Rich, Adrienne, Albert Gelpi, and Barbara C. Gelpi. *Adrienne Rich's Poetry: Texts of the Poems ; the Poet on Her Work ; Reviews and Criticism*. New York: Norton. Print.

INDEX

accessing, 17, 39-41
acknowledged, 47, 93
actively, 11, 46
adapted, 3
address, 5, 14-15, 20, 28, 30-31, 39, 47
   addressed, 4, 11-12, 20, 29-30, 46, 94
aesthetic qualities, 41
aloud, 16, 32, 43, 47, 93, 95-96
amberized, 23
April, 4
articulate, 22
artifact, 16, 19, 32, 47
audible, 43
authentic, 28-29, 33, 41
bond, 31-33
breathless gasps, 20, 28
captured, 39, 43
Caruth, Cathy, 15, 18, 20, 22, 28, 31
catastrophic, 7, 9
cathartic, 43
Celan, Paul, 30
class, 29-30
Clorinda, 21, 23, 32
cognitive, 11, 26, 46
collaborate, 3, 5, 12, 30-31, 33, 39, 43-44, 48, 90, 95
   collaborative pairing, 13
   collaborative witnessing, 30-31
collective, 3-4, 7-10, 22
combine, 5, 33, 44
comfortable, 91, 95-96
compartmentalization, 4
compassion, 33, 43, 96
compiled, 3-4, 7, 10, 13, 22
confusion, 4, 25, 91
connected, 92-93, 96
connectivity, 7
conscious, 16, 19-20, 27
consciousness, 9, 27, 104

create, 5, 11-15, 19, 25, 27, 31-34, 37, 39, 44, 46-47, 93-94
crippled, 61, 63
cry, 15, 20-23, 25-26, 28, 32, 34, 39-41, 48
cryptographer, 33
cryptonymic, 29
deconstruct, 3, 44, 46
demand, 18, 20, 23, 31
departure, 28, 43
digital, 4, 10
dimensions, 17
directly, 18, 28, 32
disconnect, 29-30
distress, 12, 43
Dream journals, 19
dreams, 12, 18-19, 23, 27, 61, 63
Eliot, T.S., 3-4, 31
embarrassment, 22
emotion
emotionally, 12, 19, 40
empathy, 28-29
encode, 9, 17, 23, 25-26, 34, 48
environment, 39-40
epic, 21
epicenters, 9
equality, 14
escape, 4, 7
event, 3-4, 7-10, 12, 15, 17-20, 22, 24-27, 29, 39-40
examination, 15-16, 18-19
example, 8, 18, 29, 43, 46-47
expectation, 39
experience, 3, 7, 9, 17, 20, 22-23, 29-30, 40, 43
exploration, 12, 17-18
expose, 4, 9-10, 18, 23, 25-26, 29, 32, 34, 39-40, 43, 47, 96
express, 13, 17-18, 29, 32, 93
face, 13, 26, 33, 93

falling, 24
false response, 32
fear, 9, 22, 39, 91
feel, 12, 18, 29-34, 39-41, 43, 46-47, 89-96
Felman, Shoshana, 12, 15, 17-19, 24, 26-27, 29-30
film, 29
flash, 4, 26-27
focus, 15, 40
forbidden forest, 21
forgotten, 18
formality, 19, 41
formed, 32, 43, 55, 59
　forming a necessary response, 29
　formulate a response, 16, 31-32
foundation, 16
foundational, 7
fragment, 3-4,7-12,18,23-25,29-30,33,40
　fragmented paralysis, 31
free, 19, 23, 25, 30, 39, 47-48
free association, 19
freeing, 23, 47
Freud, Sigmund, 18, 20, 22
frightening, 43
frightful falling-mute, 24
future broken society, 3
Gerusalemme Liberata, 21
goals, 12
guilt, 34
hallucinations, 23
heap, 4, 12, 27, 31, 33
hear, 5, 15-16, 20-24, 26, 28-29, 31-34, 39, 43, 48, 89-94, 96
help, 9, 16, 30, 91-96
heap, 4, 12, 27, 31, 33
hear, 5, 15-16, 20-24, 26, 28-29, 31-34, 39, 43, 48, 89-94, 96
help, 9, 16, 30, 91-96
helpless, 30, 92
historical recognition, 7
Holman, E. Alison, 9

Holocaust, 29-30
human, 3-4, 18
　humanity, 7
identified, 29-30
image, 4-5, 7, 9-12, 17-19, 25, 27, 31, 33-34, 40, 89-90, 94, 96
　broken images, 3-5, 7, 12, 17, 31, 33-34
　impenetrable, 27
individual, 3-5, 9-14, 16, 19, 22-26, 28, 31, 33-34, 39, 46, 89
Interpretation of Dreams, 18
interview, 89
Irma Dream, 18
jobs, 12
journals, 19
judgement, 28, 39-41, 43, 47, 93
knight, 21
knowledge, 20, 26
language, 11-12, 16-20, 24, 32, 34, 41
Laub, Dori, 12, 15
layered, 3-4, 22, 25, 33
letters, 44, 46
lines, 44, 46
listen, 18, 22, 28-29, 31-32, 43, 92, 96
literary trauma theory, 3, 15-16
located, 20
longitudinal, 8
Mallarmé, Stéphane, 20
master (of poetry), 41
meaning, 3, 9, 12, 14-16, 19, 32, 34, 39, 94
media frameworks, 9
medium, 90, 95
memories, 20, 23, 25, 39-40, 90
memory, 3, 17-18, 25, 27, 34, 48, 91
　narrative memory, 26
　traumatic memory, 18, 23
mental crypt, 25-26, 47
metaphor, 16, 19

mind, 26, 40, 43, 92
moment, 22, 25, 27, 43, 91, 93-94, 96
   micro-moment, 18
   of recognition, 22
mosaic, 4-5, 10-14, 32, 34, 37, 39, 47
   mosaic response, 12, 46-47
moving picture, 7
narrative, 18, 20, 23, 28, 43
New York City, 9
nightmares, 23
openness, 17, 28
paper, 8, 30, 43
partner, 13, 31, 33, 39-40, 43, 46-47, 89-90, 92-97; *see also* collaborate
patriarchal, 7
penetrate, 4-5, 7-14, 16-34, 40-48, 90-96
Pentagon, 9
people, 4, 7, 11, 30
permeance, 17
permeate, 4-5, 8-10, 12-14, 16-34, 40-48, 90-96
person, 3, 25, 31-32, 43, 46, 90, 92-93, 95-96
personal, 3-4, 7-8, 19, 22-23, 33, 41, 43
phonemic, 29
physical, 11, 20, 40
pictures, 27
pieces, 11-12, 26
pile, 4, 9; *see also* heap
platforms, 9
poem, 3, 5, 11-13, 15-21, 23-28, 30-34, 39-41, 43-44, 46-49, 89-96
   reformulation poetry, 3, 5, 11-13, 15-16, 24, 30, 32-33, 40, 44, 46-47, 91, 93-94, 96-97
posttraumatic, 9
power, 7, 16-17, 19
present, 3, 12, 15, 48, 89

process, 3, 5, 13, 15, 17-20, 24-27, 30, 33, 37, 39, 43-44, 46-47, 89, 91, 93, 95
psyche, 3, 12, 25, 29, 47
Psychoanalysis, 12, 15, 19
psychological, 9, 11-12, 16
puncture, 22-25, 33-34
question, 26, 90-91
read, 16, 18, 30, 32, 43, 47, 92-96
reality, 7, 12-13, 17, 24
reappears, 20, 22
recall, 18, 23, 25, 40, 91
reclamation, 48
recognition, 7, 10-12, 22, 33, 48, 90, 96
recollect, 18, 23, 25-27; *see also* recall
recombined, 46; *see also* reconstruct
reconstruct, 12, 27, 33, 46
red rocks, 21, 31-32, 34
redefine, 3, 5, 11, 33-34, 48, 94
reflect, 11, 15-16, 19-20, 30, 40, 43, 46, 89
reform, 3, 5, 10-13
reformulated, 1, 3, 5, 11-16, 19, 24, 30, 32-34, 37, 39-40, 44, 46-49, 89, 91, 93-96
regeneration, 20
rejection, 39
relationships, 11, 102
release, 22, 43
remember, 26, 40-41, 43, 89-93
repair, 35, 51, 53
repeats, 12, 15, 95; *see also* repetition
repetition, 18, 22, 24-25, 29, 40, 48
replication, 10
resolution, 11, 30
respect, 25, 27
respond, 3, 5, 10-16, 28-34, 39, 43, 46-48, 91-92, 94, 96
resurrection, 25
retrieval, 26; *see also* recall
reverberate, 18, 22, 33, 43

rhetoric, 29
rhyme, 41
rhythm, 41
Rich, Adrienne, 35
risks, 30
rooted, 3, 16-17, 46
safe, 9, 25, 27, 39-40
scream, 22-24, 28, 33, 39, 43
screening, 29-30
see, 13, 25, 29, 43, 91-94, 96
seek, 12-13, 17
semantic, 26, 29
sensations, 23
sense, 4, 17, 27, 29, 32, 91, 93, 95-96
shadow, 31-32, 34
shame, 22, 34, 47
share, 7-8, 32-33, 39, 43, 90, 93, 95
shattered, 10, 12, 30
silence, 18, 24, 29, 40
Silver, Roxane Cohen, 9
smart devices, 9
social sites, 10
society, 3-4, 7
solitude, 30-31
sorrow, 21-22
space, 14, 25, 27-28, 30-31, 33-34, 39-40, 90
speech, 16, 21, 35
spoke, 16, 29, 92
spring, 3
stand out, 25, 40
stanzas, 44, 46
state, 12, 19-20, 23, 30, 47, 92
statement, 15, 27
stones, 11
story, 7, 18-19, 22, 31, 90
storytelling, 18
strength, 5, 34, 48, 89
stricken, 11-12, 24
structure, 19, 91

students, 29-30
subconscious, 13, 16, 18-19, 22, 25, 27
subjugation, 7
subway, 4
suffering, 18, 93
survivor, 22
symbolic, 26, 29
symbols, 18
sympathy, 29
Tancred, 21-23
Tasso, Torquato, 21
technology, 7-8
television, 7-9
terror, 8, 25, 61, 63
terrorist, 8-9
testifier, 20, 25-26, 28-30, 47, 89, 95; *see also* testimony
testimony, 5, 12-13, 15-20, 24-33, 39-41, 43-44, 46-47, 49
theory, 3, 15-16
therapies, 20
thought, 12, 16-18, 22, 40, 95
time, 3, 22-23, 40-41, 46-48, 89-90, 92
trauma, 1, 3-5, 7-20, 22-26, 28-34, 39-40, 46, 48, 90, 92, 94, 96
tree, 21-22, 31, 34
trust, 32, 39, 90
truth, 23, 25, 27
twentieth century, 3
twenty-first century, 3-4, 10
unaddressed, 7, 9, 12
unconscious, 19
undergrad, 29
understand, 5, 7, 12, 16, 18-20, 26-28, 31-32, 34, 39-40, 43, 46, 89, 96
uneasiness, 90
Updegraff, John A., 9
validity, 26
verbally, 43, 48

videos, 30
virality, 10
virally, 9
visibility, 7
visual, 9, 25, 91
voice, 5, 13, 18, 22-23, 31-32, 34, 40, 43, 47-48
voyeuristic, 29
vulnerability, 14, 17, 27-28, 31, 33-34, 39, 91
wars, 7
The Waste Land, 3, 31, 34
wasteland, 4
window, 4
witness, 5, 8, 12-16, 19-20, 23-25, 27-33, 39, 43-44
    bear, 13, 19, 30, 32-33
    false witness, 28-29, 32
word, 12, 18, 27, 30, 32, 44, 46, 51, 90, 93-94
world, 8-9, 16
World Trade Center (WTC), 9
wounds, 5, 11-15, 17, 19-26, 28-34, 39-41, 43, 46-48, 94
    absorbed the, 30
    access the, 5
    accessibility of one's own, 17
    crying wound, 15, 20, 39-41
    is heard and can be accessed, 20
    mental wound, 20, 22
write, 9, 12-13, 16-19, 22, 24-31, 33-34, 40-41, 43, 90-92, 95-96

BIOS

Terriann Walling holds an honours degree in English, a Bachelor's degree in Education, and a Master's Degree in English from the University of Saskatchewan. She is currently a High School teacher in Saskatoon, Saskatchewan, Canada. Her main area of study is Twentieth Century American Literature and Literary Trauma Theory with a particular interest in modernism and William Faulkner. She is a writer and a poet whose passions lie in collaborative work, both academically as well as creatively.

George Gerard is currently a Senior Product Manager in San Francisco, California. He holds a Bachelor of Arts degree in Psychology from Syracuse University. His main area of research study focused on human memory and emotion. He pursues his love of writing and art through collaborative partnership and discovery.

CPSIA information can be obtained
at www.ICGtesting.com
Printed in the USA
LVOW05s0617020617
536704LV00002B/4/P